The Congress of the United States

C H R I S T I N E T A Y L O R - B U T L E R

Children's Press®
An Imprint of Scholastic Inc.
New York Toronto London Auckland Sydney
Mexico City New Delhi Hong Kong
Danbury, Connecticut

Content Consultant

David R. Smith, PhD

Academic Adviser and

Adjunct Assistant Professor of History

University of Michigan–Ann Arbor

Reading Consultant

Linda Cornwell

Literacy Consultant

Carmel, Indiana

Library of Congress Cataloging-in-Publication Data

Taylor-Butler, Christine.
The Congress of the United States / by Christine Taylor-Butler.
    p. cm.—(A true book)
Includes bibliographical references and index.
ISBN-13: 978-0-531-12628-8 (lib. bdg.)   978-0-531-14778-8 (pbk.)
ISBN-10: 0-531-12628-5 (lib. bdg.)   0-531-14778-9 (pbk.)
1. United States. Congress—Juvenile literature. 2. United
States—Politics and government—Juvenile literature. I. Title. II. Series.
JK1025.T39 2008
328.73—dc22   2007012253

All rights reserved. Published in 2008 by Children's Press, an imprint of Scholastic Inc.
Published simultaneously in Canada. Printed in China. 62
SCHOLASTIC, CHILDREN'S PRESS, A TRUE BOOK, and associated logos are trademarks
and/or registered trademarks of Scholastic Inc.
1 2 3 4 5 6 7 8 9 10 R 17 16 15 14 13 12 11 10 09 08

Find the Truth!

Everything you are about to read is true *except* for one of the sentences on this page.

Which one is **TRUE**?

T or F The U.S. vice president is part of Congress.

T or F You have to be born in the United States to run for Congress.

Find the answer in this book.

3

Contents

THE **BIG** TRUTH!

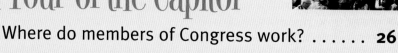

Congress declared war against 6 countries during World War II.

5 How Congress Became Congress

Who decided what Congress should look like?... **29**

6 Memorable Moments in Congress

What are some highlights
of the past 200 years? **35**

**Everett Dirksen was a Senator
from 1950 to 1969.**

5

Congress meets in the U.S. Capitol. President George Washington laid the cornerstone of the building on September 18, 1793.

CHAPTER 1

Government by the People

About 32,000 people work for Congress. Only 535 are elected officials.

The United States is a **democracy**. That means Americans vote for the people who run their government and make the laws. The part of the government that makes the laws is **Congress.**

All 535 members of Congress meet to hear the president speak.

President George W. Bush shakes hands with pages. Pages are students who help members of Congress.

The government of the United States is divided into three parts, or branches. The president is the head of the executive branch. This part of the government enforces laws. The judicial branch makes sure the laws are fair. It also settles court cases.

Congress is the **legislative**, or lawmaking, branch. This branch has the power to create and change laws. It also can create new taxes, declare war, and more. Thousands of people work together to do these jobs.

THE THREE BRANCHES OF GOVERNMENT

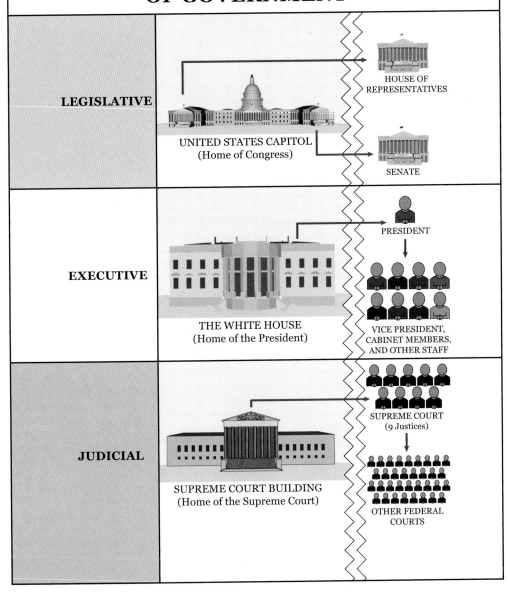

LEGISLATIVE

UNITED STATES CAPITOL
(Home of Congress)

HOUSE OF REPRESENTATIVES

SENATE

EXECUTIVE

THE WHITE HOUSE
(Home of the President)

PRESIDENT

VICE PRESIDENT, CABINET MEMBERS, AND OTHER STAFF

JUDICIAL

SUPREME COURT BUILDING
(Home of the Supreme Court)

SUPREME COURT
(9 Justices)

OTHER FEDERAL COURTS

Maxine Waters became a representative for California in 1991. California has more representatives than other states because it has the largest population.

CHAPTER 2

Welcome to the House

Who represents you in the House? Go to www.house.gov and use your zip code to find out.

Congress has two parts, or houses. One is called the House of Representatives. The other is the Senate. What happens in each of these houses?

You don't need to be born in the United States to be in Congress. But you need to be a citizen—someone who could get this passport.

PASSPORT

United States of America

11

Who's in the House?

Voters elect people to the House of Representatives. They are called **representatives**, or House members. They serve a **term** of two years.

Who can be a representative? You need to be at least 25 years old. You must have been a U.S. citizen for at least seven years. And you must run for office in the state where you live. You do not have to have been born in the United States to run for Congress.

Representatives are elected every two years. Americans must be at least 18 years old to vote.

Each House member represents about 690,000 people. States with larger populations get more members. That means big states have more power in the House. (It's different in the Senate.)

Altogether, there are 435 representatives who can vote in the House. There are also members who can't vote. They come from the U.S. Virgin Islands, Washington, D.C., American Samoa (suh-MOH-uh), Puerto Rico, and Guam (GWAHM).

Speaker of the House

Each term, the House elects a leader called the Speaker of the House. The Speaker runs the **sessions**, or formal meetings, of the House. Representatives debate, or discuss, issues before voting. The Speaker helps this debate along. He or she tells people when they can speak.

The Speaker has another important job, as well. What happens if the U.S. president and vice president can no longer serve? The Speaker becomes president!

Nancy Pelosi has been a member of the House since 1987.

The first female Speaker of the House, Nancy Pelosi of California, was elected in 2007.

In 1974, members of the House of Representatives discuss impeaching President Richard Nixon. Nixon resigned instead.

Powers of the House

Both branches of Congress work to make new laws. However, each branch has its own powers. Only the House of Representatives can create a new tax. Only members of the House can **impeach**, or bring charges against, a president for breaking a law. Another power of the House is to break a tie vote in a presidential election.

Wild horses live in western states such as Montana and Nevada.

The House Committee on Natural Resources approved a bill to protect America's wild horses in 2007.

Representatives break into smaller groups to manage all their work. They form about 20 groups called **committees**. The committees meet to talk about ideas. They write **bills,** or written plans of new laws.

From Idea to Law

How does an idea turn into a law? Here's an example.

1. The Idea

Some students want a law requiring schools to recycle. They write a letter to their representative or senator.

2. Sponsorship

The representative agrees to support the idea. She writes a bill.

With or without a law, your school can start a recycling program.

3. Committee Review

A committee reviews the bill. Its members can make changes.

4. The Vote

The bill passes if more than half of the representatives vote for it.

5. The Other Branch

The bill moves on to the other house. Both houses must approve it.

6. Veto or Law?

The president has two choices. He can say no, or veto the bill. This bill could still become a law—if two out of every three members of Congress approve it.

Or, the president can say yes and sign the bill. Now it becomes a law. Every school in the country must recycle!

Charles Schumer and Hillary Clinton are the two U.S. senators from New York. Find out who your senators are at www.senate.gov.

CHAPTER 3

Step Into the Senate

Senators used to get a quill pen on their desks. Now they get two pencils.

The Senate has 100 members. They are called **senators**. Senators serve six-year terms. Large and small states elect the same number of senators. Each state has two. That means all states have equal power in the Senate.

Who Can Be a Senator?

It is a little harder to become a senator than a representative. There are fewer senators. Senators must be at least 30 years old. They must have been U.S. citizens for at least nine years. Senators must also live in the state they represent.

The vice president is the leader of the Senate. However, the vice president votes only to break a tie. Senators elect another leader known as the president pro tempore. The words *pro tempore* mean "for the time being" in Latin. The president pro tempore may lead Senate sessions.

Robert Dole served in the Senate from 1969 to 1996.

Special Powers

Senators have powers that representatives don't have. The U.S. president picks or appoints some judges, cabinet members, and other officials. The Senate must vote to confirm or reject these officials. Senators also approve agreements with foreign countries.

Senator Barack Obama attends a meeting of the Senate Foreign Relations Committee.

The Senate has 16 committees. The Foreign Relations Committee helps the president deal with other nations. The Finance Committee helps decide how the government should spend its money. Other committees handle issues such as education, farming, and energy.

The Library of Congress is the largest library in the world. Its books, recordings, maps, and photographs are available to members of Congress, as well as the public.

CHAPTER 4

A Government That Works

The Library of Congress contains the world's largest collection of comic books—100,000 issues!

How does Congress get its work done? Mostly that happens in meetings. There are committee meetings. And there are larger meetings of the whole group. Congress meets in the U.S. Capitol in Washington, D.C.

Kinds of Sessions

Most sessions, or meetings, are open to the public. Sometimes the members vote to go into a closed session. This happens when the members discuss information they want to keep secret.

The House of Representatives and the Senate sometimes meet together. This is called a joint session. Joint sessions happen on special occasions, such as when the president gives the State of the Union address.

The president speaks to both houses of Congress at least once a year. This speech is called the State of the Union address.

Members of Congress earn $165,200 each year.

Representatives vote on many issues. Voting results are often displayed on an electronic board above the room.

A Job with Privileges

Members of Congress get special privileges that other citizens don't get. They cannot be arrested for small crimes. This might sound unfair. But this rule was put in place to keep political enemies from accusing each other of little crimes.

Members have special license plates for their cars, too. They are allowed to park for free, even at the airport. The plates also let police officers know that the car's owner is a member of Congress.

The House meets in the south wing.

The Senate meets in the north wing.

United States Capitol

The congressional building shares its name with the surrounding area.

United States Supreme Court

Before this building was completed in 1935, the Supreme Court met in the basement of the Capitol.

About the Capitol

The Capitol covers 4 acres (1.6 hectares) and contains 540 rooms.

From the basement to the top of the dome, there are 365 steps.

The inside of the Capitol's dome is called the rotunda. It is 96 feet (29 meters) across. It's used for important ceremonies.

North
South
East
West

A Tour of the Capitol

Congress's home is the U.S. Capitol in Washington, D.C.
Take a tour of the neighborhood!

This round building honors the third U.S. president, Thomas Jefferson.

This building was built to honor the 16th president, Abraham Lincoln. It was modeled after a Greek temple.

The U.S. president has lived and worked here since 1800.

More than 23 million people a year visit these museums. They can choose among art museums, the Air and Space Museum, the National Museum of Natural History, and more.

This 555-foot (169-meter)-tall structure is a symbol of George Washington's huge influence on the United States.

Jefferson Memorial

Smithsonian

Washington Monument

White House

Lincoln Memorial

Potomac River

Tidal Basin

Reflecting Pool

The British version of Congress is called Parliament (PAR-luh-muhnt). In this illustration, King George III opens Parliament. King George III and the Parliament ruled the colonies during the Revolutionary War.

CHAPTER 5

How Congress Became Congress

The British Parliament was a model for the U.S. Congress. Both have two houses.

The United States declared itself independent from Great Britain in 1776. But it didn't have a government! State leaders met to create a government in 1787. They decided how the new government would be organized. They wrote the most important laws for the new country. They did it with a document called the **Constitution**.

Writing a Constitution

The states' leaders had a great deal to debate. The representative from Virginia suggested a plan. The plan divided the government into three branches. Congress makes up one of these branches. Larger states wanted to have more power in Congress. Smaller states wanted every state to have an equal number of votes.

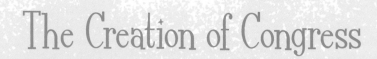

The Creation of Congress

1775 ➡
The Revolutionary War begins.

1781 ➡
An early U.S. constitution, called the Articles of Confederation, becomes law.

1783 ➡
The Revolutionary War ends.

So what would the new Congress be like? The leaders found a solution that would make both large and small states content. They divided Congress into two houses. One house, the House of Representatives, would give the big states more voting power. The other, the Senate, would give an equal number of votes to each state.

1788 ➡ **1789**

Enough states approve the Constitution for it to become the law of the land.

The first session of Congress meets.

1787 ➡

The Constitutional Convention meets to write the U.S. Constitution.

In March of 1789, Congress began its first day of work under the Constitution. Finally, the United States had a Congress—and a government. Today, the same system of government that was created more than 200 years ago is still in use.

Congress grew as the U.S. population increased during the 1800s. The Capitol grew as well. It even got a new dome.

A Seat in the Senate

There are many traditions surrounding the desks that senators use. Today, 100 desks fill the Senate chamber. Each senator is assigned a specific desk.

In 1965, a senator began keeping candy in his desk. He shared his stash with his fellow senators. Since then, every senator assigned to that desk has kept up the tradition. It's always stocked with treats!

For nearly 100 years, senators have been carving their names into the drawers of their assigned desks. If you want to know which senators have sat at a desk, just look in the drawer!

Senate candy desk

Senators' names inside a drawer

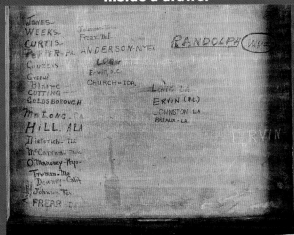

Everett Dirksen was a member of the House for 16 years and a member of the Senate for 19. He worked hard to pass the 1964 Civil Rights Act, which he helped to write.

CHAPTER 6

Memorable Moments in Congress

In 2007, Keith Ellison of Minnesota became the first Muslim elected to Congress.

Congress has played an important role in U.S. history. Its members have declared war, protected people's rights, and much more. Here are a few examples of some of Congress's powerful decisions.

U.S. representative Keith Ellison takes his oath of office by swearing on a Qur'an (kor-AHN), the Muslim holy book. This copy of the Qur'an was owned by Thomas Jefferson.

Removing a President from Office

Congress has the power to remove a president from office. Congress can use this power only if a president commits a serious crime.

The process of removing a president from power begins with impeachment, or accusation. Impeachment is such a serious step that Congress has only taken it twice. The first time was in 1868. Andrew Johnson was president.

This illustration shows the House of Representatives voting on whether or not to impeach President Johnson. They voted to impeach him.

Tickets to Johnson's impeachment trial were very popular!

Johnson and Congress disagreed about major issues. Congress took steps to limit Johnson's power. He was told that he couldn't fire any officials unless Congress approved. Johnson didn't listen. He fired his secretary of war. Congress used this as a reason to get rid of Johnson.

The House voted to impeach Johnson. He went on trial in the Senate. It was a power struggle between the president and Congress. Everyone wanted to know who would win.

It would not be easy to remove Johnson from office. Two out of every three senators would need to vote against him. They came up short by only one vote! Johnson kept his job.

President Roosevelt asks Congress to declare war against Japan after the attack on Pearl Harbor.

Declaring War

December 7, 1941, is a day Americans will never forget. Japanese pilots attacked a U.S. naval base. The base was in Pearl Harbor, Hawaii. They killed more than 2,300 American soldiers and sailors in less than two hours. They damaged or destroyed about 19 U.S. ships and 180 airplanes.

The next day, President Franklin D. Roosevelt spoke to a joint session of Congress. Most Americans listened to the speech on the radio. Roosevelt urged Congress to declare war on Japan.

Right after Roosevelt spoke, the Senate voted to declare war. Every senator voted for it. The House voted to go to war 12 minutes later.

The Constitution gives Congress the power to declare war. Congress has formally declared war only five times. (But Congress has approved the use of force against other countries many times. This action often results in a war, too. This is what happened with respect to the Iraq War.)

Only one representative voted against World War II.

Representative Jeannette Rankin voted against joining World War II. She explained, "As a woman, I can't go to war and I refuse to send anyone else."

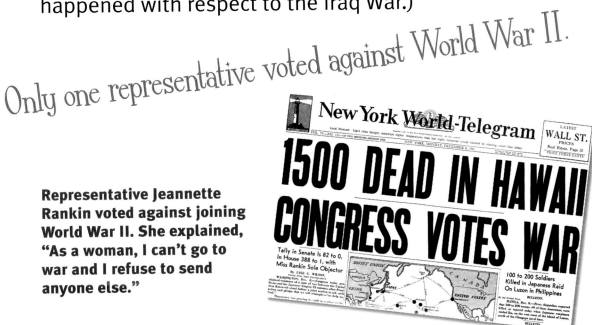

Overcoming Problems

In 1957, a senator spoke to the Senate for 24 hours and 18 minutes. Senator Strom Thurmond stopped talking only when his doctor threatened to drag him off the floor. Had the senator lost his mind? No. He was trying to block a bill from becoming law.

The House and Senate must both agree on a bill before it can be sent to the president. Sometimes a member of the Senate is unhappy with a bill. He or she can try to prevent a vote by staging a **filibuster**. A filibuster is one long, long speech. Thurmond's filibuster is the longest in U.S. history.

Strom Thurmond was an outspoken opponent of the Civil Rights Act. In 1957, he staged a filibuster in the Senate. He read aloud from the Declaration of Independence to fill the time.

John Lewis (far right) became a U.S. representative in 1986. Here, he marches in support of better voting rights for African Americans, in 1965. With him (left to right) are Ralph Abernathy, James Forman, Martin Luther King Jr., and Jesse Douglas.

Thurmond was trying to prevent the **Civil Rights** Act of 1957 from becoming a law. This law would protect African Americans' right to vote.

Most members of Congress supported the act. They did not give up. When Thurmond finally stopped speaking, the senate voted and the act passed! President Eisenhower signed the act and it became law.

A Model Congress

The members of the House of Representatives and the Senate are elected by and for the people. They work hard to make laws that protect people's rights, safety, and well-being. The U.S. Congress was formed more than 200 years ago. Today, it remains a model for countries all over the world. ★

Don't forget—members of Congress work for the American people!

Congress created by: Article I, Section I, of the U.S. Constitution

First meeting of Congress: March 4, 1789

Requirements to be a senator: At least 30 years old; a U.S. citizen for 9 years

Requirements to be a representative: At least 25 years old; a U.S. citizen for 7 years

Length of one term in the Senate: 6

Length of one term in the House: 2

Number of senators in the first Congress: 26

Number of representatives in the first Congress: 65

Number of senators today: 100

Number of representatives today: 435

Did you find the truth?

T The U.S. vice president is part of Congress.

F You have to be born in the United States to run for Congress.

Resources

Books

Feldman, Ruth Tenzer. *How Congress Works: A Look at the Legislative Branch.* Minneapolis: Lerner Publications, 2004.

Giddens-White, Byron. *Congress and the Legislative Branch.* Chicago: Heinemann Library, 2006.

Heath, David. *The Congress of the United States.* Mankato, MN: Capstone Press, 1999.

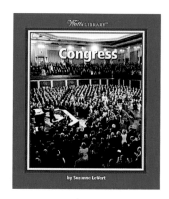

LeVert, Suzanne. *The Congress.* Danbury, CT: Franklin Watts, 2005.

McElroy, Lisa Tucker. *Nancy Pelosi: First Woman Speaker of the House.* Minneapolis: Lerner Publishing, 2008.

Murphy, Patricia J. *The U.S. Congress.* Minneapolis: Compass Point Books, 2002.

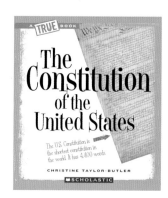

Sanders, Mark C. *Congress.* Austin: Steadwell Books, 2000.

Taylor-Butler, Christine. *The Constitution of the United States.* Danbury, CT: Children's Press, 2008.

Organizations and Web Sites

Explore Parliament

www.explore.parliament.uk

Learn more about the history of the British Parliament.

Office of the Clerk: Kids in the House

clerkkids.house.gov/Congress/members/first_day/index.html

Find out what happens on the first day of Congress.

United States House of Representatives

www.house.gov

See what's happening on the House floor this week.

United States Senate

www.senate.gov

Find your two U.S. senators.

Places to Visit

The House of Representatives

Washington, DC 20515

202-224-3121

www.house.gov

See the House chamber and office buildings.

The U.S. Senate

Washington, DC 20510

202-224-3121

www.senate.gov

Watch the Senate in session.

Important Words

bills – written plans of new laws

civil rights – individual rights and freedoms given to all citizens by law

committees – groups of people who speak for a larger group

Congress – the highest lawmaking body of the United States, made up of the Senate and the House of Representatives

Constitution (kon-stuh-TOO-shun) – the 1787 document that explains the people's rights and the U.S. government's powers

democracy (di-MAW-kruh-see) – a government that is elected by the people

filibuster (FI-luh-BUS-tuhr) – a long speech by a senator to delay a vote

impeach – to bring charges against a public official for a crime

legislative (le-juhs-LAY-tiv) – related to the branch of government that makes laws; Congress is the legislative branch

representatives – people elected to listen and speak for other people; members of the House of Representatives

senators – people elected to serve in a lawmaking body; members of the U.S. Senate

sessions – formal meetings

term – the set length of time that an elected official serves in office

Index

About the Author

Christine Taylor-Butler has written more than 30 books for children. She has written several books in the True Books American History series, including *The Bill of Rights*, *The Constitution*, *Explorers of North America*, *The Supreme Court*, and *The Presidency*.

A native of Ohio, Taylor-Butler now lives in Kansas City, Missouri, with her husband, Ken, and their two daughters. She holds degrees in both civil engineering and art and design from the Massachusetts Institute of Technology.